Old STEWARTON, DUNLOP and

by
Susan Milligan

This early 1960s view of Stewarton from the south east, taken from Gameshill, shows the spinning and dyeing factory of Thomas Mackie and Sons in the foreground. The spire of John Knox Church can be seen in the distance on the left, and Cairns Church, further along the High Street, near the centre. Cairns Church was established as a United Presbyterian Church in 1776 at Bridgend, and the Rev. Peter Cairns was minister from 1827; in 1854 the new building was erected in the High Street, and became known as Cairns United Free Church in his honour in 1900. It rejoined the Church of Scotland at the union of churches some years later, and the congregation joined that of the Parish Church (St Columba's) in 1961. A few years later Cairns Church was demolished. The three-storey building to the right of Cairns Church is Nairn's hosiery factory in Springwell Place, now converted into flats.

© Susan Milligan, 2001
First published in the United Kingdom, 2001,
by Stenlake Publishing, Ochiltree Sawmill, The Lade,
Ochiltree, Ayrshire, KA18 2NX
Telephone/Fax: 01290 423114
enquiries@stenlake.co.uk

www.stenlake.co.uk

ISBN 1 84033 143 7

ACKNOWLEDGEMENTS
I would like to thank the people of Stewarton, Dunlop and Lugton who willingly helped me with my enquiries in the course of writing this book, in particular Mr Robert Watt of Past and Present, Stewarton, Mr Alastair Barclay, Mr and Mrs Tom Mackie, Miss Ada McLachlan, Barbara Wiseman, Mrs Jean Sim and Mr and Mrs Angus Robertson. I derived useful information from articles in programmes of the Stewarton Bonnet Guild's annual festival, many of them written by Alastair Barclay, and also from his articles in the *Kilmarnock Standard*. I am grateful to the staff of Stewarton Library, the Dick Institute, Kilmarnock, the Carnegie Library, Ayr, and the Mitchell Library, Glasgow, for their help.

SOME FURTHER READING
The books listed below were used by the author during her research. None of them are available from Stenlake Publishing. Those interested in finding out more are advised to contact their local bookshop or reference library.

The Statistical Account of Scotland, Vol. VI, 1791–1799.
The New Statistical Account of Scotland, Vol. V, 1845.
The Third Statistical Account of Scotland: Ayrshire, 1951.
Alastair Barclay, *The Bonnet Toun*, Stewarton Bonnet Guild, 1989.
John F. Bayne, *Dunlop Parish: a History of Church, Parish, and Nobility*, Edinburgh, 1935.
Andrew Boyle, *Ayrshire Heritage*, Ayrshire, 1990.
Dugald Campbell (ed.), *Dunlop Ancient and Modern Exhibition, 27–29 March 1998*, Dunlop Public Hall.
Jack House, *Stewarton*, Stewarton Bonnet Guild, *c*.1970

Lainshaw Street was one of Stewarton's most busy thoroughfares, crowded with small shops, cottages and tenements, the most famous of which was Happyland, built to house factory workers. The buildings at the near left are gone, replaced by modern houses, and beyond them, just past the break in the row where the Social Club now stands, was a shop owned by Aitchison the chemist. Just past it was Bella Boyd's fish and chip shop (previously Willie Barclay's). Across the road was Barclay the butcher and near it the Bank. Between this and the small house jutting out (which still stands), the houses in this picture were replaced by the red sandstone Aitchison's Building and next to it a red sandstone tenement erected in 1936 and known as the Queen Mary Building in honour of the ship launched in that year.

INTRODUCTION

There has been a church and settlement at Stewarton since medieval times. In the late thirteenth century the land became the property of the High Stewards of Scotland, who started the line of the Stewart family. It was probably around this time that the township of Stewarton came into being.

During the sixteenth century the first of the notorious feuds of Ayrshire, fought between the Montgomeries of Eglinton and the Cunninghames of Kilmaurs, sparked off many violent incidents in this part of the country. Meanwhile the townspeople of Stewarton had been going about their business, chief among which was the knitting of bonnets. It was probably in 1590 that the bonnet makers constituted themselves into a corporation to control the cottage industry and guarantee standards. The Bonnet Court of Corsehill, as it was known, was presided over by the Laird of Corsehill. The principal markets were the local fairs held in most towns; Stewarton had three annual fairs. Thirty years later the bonnet makers of Stewarton succeeded in breaking into the very much larger market of Glasgow, by signing what became known in Stewarton as the 'Great Agreement'. The signatories were the Laird of Corsehill and the Deacon Heritable of the Bonnet Court, Sir Alexander Cunninghame, and his counterpart in Glasgow, Gavin Naismith, Deacon of the Incorporation of Bonnetmakers and Dyers of Glasgow. The Laird of Corsehill undertook to guarantee the supply and quality of all bonnets produced in Stewarton, being liable to a sizeable fine if a complaint were upheld, and in return the members of Stewarton's Bonnet Court were given the right 'in all tyme coming to haunt the mercats of Glasgow to sell their bonnets without ony interruptions to be maid to their guds being visited and sichtet [inspected]'. This firmly established Stewarton as a viable competitor in the important market of Glasgow and gave it an advantage over neighbouring Kilmarnock. The privileges of a share in the Glasgow market, and the opportunity for selling bonnets on from there to all parts of Scotland, were jealously guarded, and the Bonnet Court was rigorous in laying down the law on such matters as the weight of bonnets and the quality of workmanship and dyes. Supply was carefully controlled too, and when the market was in danger of being flooded, occasional cessations of work, or 'idlesetts', were imposed.

It was rather ironic that in spite of the town's strong weaving community, Stewarton's most famous son, David Dale, born in 1739, set up his cotton and linen mills not in Stewarton but in New Lanark and other places. The first *Statistical Account* of 1791 reported that there were more than a hundred weavers in the town and fifty years later the New Statistical Account stated that there were about 300 weavers in cotton and silk. Bonnet making was still very important and after Stewarton's first bonnet factory was set up in 1820, soon followed by others, the industry moved out of cottages and into factories. The allied trades of dyeing and spinning were established in mills on the banks of the town's many burns, and there were also woollen mills and factories making spindles for the mills. Stewarton also made steel clockwork, exported as far as America, and tiles and bricks.

As bonnets ceased to be the universal Scottish headgear, the factories diversified into other types of knitwear and clothing. Several innovations in manufacturing were established in Stewarton and although most of the firms were quite small, this progressive approach to mechanisation and design served the town well and provided plenty of employment. Around the start of the twentieth century various kinds of knitted outerwear and underwear were introduced. When Sherpa Tenzing set foot on Everest with Sir Edmund Hillary, he was wearing a balaclava made in Stewarton. The tradition of craftsmanship, ability to adapt to the demands of the market, and proximity to Glasgow are three reasons why knitwear factories continued to be major employers in Stewarton for such a long time, and some clothing, including Scotland's supply of regimental bonnets, is still made in the town. In the mid-twentieth century some light engineering was established, with factories making engine parts and precision cutting tools for aircraft companies and other types of engineering.

Stewarton has long been a centre of dairy agriculture, but the parish of Dunlop to the north eclipsed its larger neighbour in this respect, giving its name to a type of whole-milk cheese introduced in the late seventeenth century which became so popular that the name Dunlop was applied to cheese made in the same style in many other districts. Cheese cadgers, or dealers, set up business in the village, and it became a centre of trade as well as production. Most Ayrshire farms produced Dunlop cheese and in the late eighteenth and early nineteenth centuries this became a mainstay of Ayrshire's rural economy. Farmhouse cheeses continued to be produced throughout Ayrshire until the Second World War. The whey that was left over from cheese making was used to feed pigs, and a small high-quality bacon-curing industry grew up in Dunlop, with Ayrshire bacon gaining a very high reputation throughout the country.

Dunlop also became famous for its cattle. Thanks to agricultural improvements introduced by landowners, including John Dunlop of Dunlop, by the mid-eighteenth century a new breed of dairy cattle was being produced here, first known as Dunlop, and then as Cunninghame cows, and later, as their fame spread, as Ayrshire cows. The success of this highly productive breed was such that it was adopted throughout the world.

There was a settlement and church at Dunlop from the thirteenth century, and the family of Dunlop has been traced back to 1260. In the mid-seventeenth century there was a small cluster of houses around the church, which was rebuilt in the eighteenth and again in the nineteenth century. The village grew during that time with the construction first of Townfoot and then of Main Street.

Dunlop and Lugton in the nineteenth century were home to five corn mills, three grain merchants, a sawmill, several joiners and builders, a gas works, two creameries, six blacksmiths, several quarries and a blanket mill. The most important business in Dunlop was Robert Howie and Sons, which was set up in 1850 and expanded from a joinery and cartwright's business into grain and timber, sawmilling, agricultural machinery, animal feeds and feed mills, lime processing, frozen food and farm fencing. The firm remains in business in Dunlop, with several branches in other locations.

The railway link with Glasgow and Kilmarnock, established in 1873, was vital for the prosperity of most of these rural industries. Lugton, an important crossroads at the north end of the parish, leading to Beith, Irvine, Barrhead and Dunlop, had in addition a rail line to Ardrossan which opened in 1888. After iron ore was discovered here in the mid-nineteenth century, Lugton grew from a collection of four buildings – an inn, a smithy, and two toll houses – to a little community centred on the iron ore mine and later, when this was worked out, brickworks. Long before iron ore was mined there, lime was quarried and processed at Lugton; although the local supply has been worked out, there is still a limeworks, now owned by Robert Howie and Sons of Dunlop. The limeworks is the only industry in Lugton to have survived the closure of the railway in the 1960s and all the small businesses have gone too.

In this unusual view of the Corsehillbanks and Dean Street end of Stewarton, the Corsehill Burn in the foreground rushes down to meet the Annick on the other side of the High Street (off the right hand side of this picture). The picture is taken from the high path on the right bank of the burn, not far inside the gates of the Cunningham Watt Memorial Park, which was gifted to the town by Miss Cunningham Watt to commemorate Dr John Cunningham. Perched on the opposite bank of the burn, on the far left of this picture, is the old Fever Hospital, now a private house, fronting on to Bowes Rigg. Between it and the burn a mill lade, drawn off from the dam further up the burn, carries water down to the Corsehill Mill, a corn mill which stood near where the burn flowed under the High Street. Nearer the mill, the lade was carried on an aqueduct; the part of the lade in the picture is now the route of the footpath on the left side of the burn. Looking across towards Dean Street (a view which is now obscured by the many trees which have grown up here) Russell's bonnet factory, now demolished, can be seen on the far right. The other factory is Alexander's, a knitwear and hosiery works. It is now the Riverford factory and although altered, is still recognisable.

Kirkford is named after the ford on the Annick which people crossed on their way to the Kirk. This view from the early 1960s is taken from the Kilmarnock road. On the right is Loudon Street, and beyond it can be seen 'Mackie's lum', the chimney of Thomas Mackie and Sons' Bridgend Mills. Thomas Mackie came to Stewarton from Drummore in 1823 with a barrow of dyes and feathers. At the time there were fifty bonnet makers in Stewarton and Mackie set up a business dyeing the yarn and the feathers that decorated the bonnets. Later he started a spinning mill and his factory became one of the largest, and the most long-lived, in Stewarton. At 165 feet, the chimney was at one time the highest in Ayrshire and aircraft navigators used to take their bearings from it. It was lowered (before this picture was taken) when the replacement of solid fuel by oil made its great height redundant. Thomas had two sons, Thomas and Robert; the former carried on the family business, but in 1842 the latter started up a separate business of his own, manufacturing bonnets and hosiery at the Annickvale Works in Holm Street. He later also set up a spinning mill.

Thomas Mackie of Hapland, Dunlop, the grandson of Thomas who set up the dyeing and spinning firm, moved the Stewarton works to the site at Bridgend and was joined in his business by his younger brother, James. This view, taken in the late 1970s, shows the famous chimney with the Cuts Burn in the foreground. The factories on the left are the Bridgend works of John Currie, Son and Co. Currie's was started in 1868 and made Stewarton bonnets, glengarries and balmorals. Their balaclavas were exported to India where they were used in the hill stations. They later specialised in knitwear, particularly cashmere and camel hair scarves, and the bonnet making stopped. After a couple of takeovers the family connection with the firm came to an end in 1969, but the firm carried on under the same name. The factory was later occupied by Domino's, who ceased trading in 2000.

The back road at Bridgend, showing Mackie's lum. In the 1960s Thomas (T.W.) Mackie, great-grandson of the founder of the company, ran the business and by the end of that decade production was mainly dyed yarn for the carpet industry, with some also for the hosiery trade. Thomas Mackie and Sons also incorporated Hapland Mills, Dunlop, and Craigend Mills, Kilmarnock. In 1983 Robert Mackie and Co. was bought by its 'brother' company, 140 years after it had been founded. The firm continues to make hats, scarves and bonnets at Bridgend, in premises across the road from their old factory which can be seen in the centre of this photograph.

Dean Street, looking north east to the Darlington Bridge over the East Burn and on up the Old Glasgow Road. Dean Street (originally Deans Street), known as Daurlintoon or Darlingtown to its inhabitants, was a close-knit working community and almost a village apart. Tenements were built by the factory owners in the town to house their workers and 'the Castle' in Dean Street, among the buildings on the extreme right of this picture, was one of the most famous. Deans Street was named after William Deans, a lawyer who along with other men opened wool and worsted mills at Robertland, and also founded a large carpet factory and later a brick and tile works. He died in 1828, aged 49.

The High Street in the early twentieth century. The small road opening on the right is Springwell Place where John Nairn had his knitwear factory; his house is the one on this corner. Next to it is the Eagle Inn with its stone eagle mounted above the doorway. In the early twentieth century there was a string of public houses and inns all the way from 'Punt' Welsh's at the foot of Lainshaw Street, to Minnie Cochrane's at Dean Street. The others included the Auld Hoose and the Railway Hotel further up Lainshaw Street, the Balmoral Bar and John Newland's Bar in Main Street, and the Palace Bar in High Street. In 1920, after a poll of the townspeople, Stewarton's temperance movement succeeded in stopping the sale of alcohol in every one and the landlords had to convert their premises to cafes and ice-cream shops. It was not until 1961 that the town voted to permit the sale of alcohol again.

The first *Statistical Account* of the 1790s says that 'the town of Stewarton may vie with any of its size in the west of Scotland, for beauty, regularity, and cleanness. It consists of one long and broad street, with a cross one.' The High Street is dominated by the John Knox Church, whose spire can be seen here. It was built in 1841, after a breakaway group from the Kirk, which had for many years met without church premises of their own, founded the New Church at the top of Avenue Street (later the Congregational Church). Bitter disputes led to their losing this church and they eventually managed to purchase land in the High Street to build a new one, despite the efforts of William Cuninghame (the younger) of Lainshaw to prevent it. Legal action by Cuninghame to prevent this congregation from being incorporated into the Church of Scotland resulted in the celebrated Stewarton Case. This led to the Disruption of 1843 which split the established Church of Scotland in two. Cuninghame tried to reclaim this new High Street church for the Church of Scotland, but after a legal battle failed to do so and the congregation was the only Free Church in Scotland which held on to its building. It was later named the John Knox Church and in 1929 was reunited with the established church.

Avenue Street, Stewarton

Avenue Street was planned and laid out in the late eighteenth century as a grand approach to the Cuninghames' estate and mansion at Corsehill. It was never completed, but it was soon after this that the Cuninghame Institute was built by the Cuninghame family. For a time William Cuninghame (the younger) of Lainshaw ran a school in it which was known as the Academy. In 1877 the town council took it over as a town hall and held a bazaar to raise funds for its conversion. It was opened as the Institute Hall in 1878 by Sir William Cunninghame of Corsehill, MP for Ayr Burgh, and it was formally gifted to the council by the family in 1928. It contained halls and a committee room, and the entrance was from Avenue Street. The large hall on the ground floor was used for billiards, carpet bowls and dominoes, and was known as the Club. When the library opened in the Institute in the 1950s, the Club was closed and a small hall at the rear was given over to the members as 'the old men's cabin'. In 1981 this was incorporated into the library and a new extension was built for the Club.

This view of the Cross, *c*.1951, shows Stewarton to be a busy and thriving town. There were at least fifty small shops in the town. Cochrane's Hotel (now demolished) was at the corner of Lainshaw and Rigg Streets, and next to it was Cochrane's grocery shop (which is just seen here on the extreme left). Across the road is the Misses Watt Browns' millinery and dressmaking business, and on the corner Liddell and Gillies the bakers. On the opposite corner of Vennel Street is Smith's newsagents. Further down this side, on part of the same site as the present Co-op, was the Kilmarnock Equitable Co-operative Society, Stewarton's largest shop, and purveyor of all sorts of household items and groceries. The Co-op was founded in Kilmarnock in 1844 and a branch was set up in Stewarton's Avenue Square around 1890. By 1904 it had moved to this site in Main Street.

'Welsh's corner' of Lainshaw Street, looking towards the Cross, is almost unrecognisable as today's Deans Corner with its mini-roundabout. Peter ('Punt') Welsh's public house is at the corner of the row on the near left of the picture. (The building before it, at the extreme left, belonged to Andrew Deans, painter and decorator.) The path leading to the Auld Kirk (St Columba's) is at the far right. Welsh's closed before Stewarton went 'dry' in 1921 and became an ice-cream shop. Herds of cows and flocks of sheep were a common sight in the streets in the old days. Drovers used to take their animals from markets in Kilmarnock to butchers in Stewarton, who slaughtered them in their back shops.

The house on the far right of the previous picture is seen on the far left of this one, and is where the church hall stands now. The Y symbol on the end wall of the Auld Kirk is a well-known Stewarton emblem, representing the shake fork which figures in the old story of how Malcolm Canmore escaped from the murderous Macbeth. It is said that Malcolm was fleeing across the fields at Corsehill and took refuge in a hayrick, pleading with the farmer to fork over more hay to conceal him, which is where the motto 'Over Fork Over' comes from. The church clock was made in Stewarton, which had a clockwork factory in the early nineteenth century. The white building on the right once housed the parish school.

The Auld Kirk was built in 1696. At that time the spire was in the centre of the building, but it was altered in 1730 and again in 1772 when the roof was taken off and the walls heightened. It was enlarged again in 1825 by being widened on the north side. For many years it was known as the Laigh Kirk and in 1961 it incorporated the congregation of the Cairns Church and became known as St Columba's. The oldest authenticated stone in the kirkyard is dated 1676 and reads: 'Here lies the Corps of Andrew Robertson, innkeeper in Stewarton'. An uncle of Robert Burns, also named Robert Burns, is buried here; he used to help guard the kirkyard in the time of the bodysnatchers.

Lainshaw Mill, a corn mill, and its adjoining house sat on the Annick right by the viaduct, and the rowan tree growing up the chimney was a source of fascination for travellers on the line. It became very much bigger before the house was demolished in the second half of the twentieth century. The mill was powered by a lade drawn off the Annick which was dammed further up at Kirkford. For many decades the mill was worked by the Eaglesham family; it ceased grinding corn in the 1930s. The viaduct has a 500 feet span and ten arches, the highest of which is 100 feet tall. It is an impressive feat of architectural engineering, but its construction cost the lives of two labourers who were killed while working on it. Both men were 28 years old and they are buried in St Columba's churchyard where a stone was erected to their memory.

The toll house on the road to Kilmarnock in the March snow. The Lainshaw Viaduct can be seen in the background. There were also toll houses on the road to Irvine and on the Glasgow road.

The Lainshaw gates used to have the jawbone of a whale over the central gate. William Cuninghame, a Glasgow tobacco merchant, spent large sums of money improving the Lainshaw estate, which he had leased from the Montgomerie family on the basis that when they redeemed it they would reimburse him for all the improvements he made. Cuninghame's fortunes soared when he bought up tobacco during a slump and resold it at seven times the price. He was able to pour money into the estate and the Montgomeries, who had lost their money in the American War of Independence, were never able to regain it. Cuninghame instructed the builders of the gates: 'Make them so they'll stand frae here till the Day of Judgement.' Although that day has not yet come, the gates are gone, removed to make way for a wider road into a housing scheme built in the 1950s. The gate houses, however, still stand. The one on the right had latterly been used by the Lainshaw estate's gardener, and the one on the left by the chauffeur.

The Lainshaw estate was taken over by William Cuninghame the younger in 1804. Throughout the first half of the nineteenth century the house was extensively rebuilt in various architectural styles. Cuninghame was at the centre of upheavals in the religious life of Stewarton in the nineteenth century which turned out to have far-reaching consequences. He began a legal battle with the Church of Scotland (known as 'the Stewarton Case') to deny them the power to form new congregations in 'quoad sacra' parishes. When the House of Lords threw out the Church's case in 1843, many dissenting ministers walked out of the Church of Scotland, an event known as the Disruption. Cuninghame spent his life in a state of preparation for the Second Coming. It is said that on certain occasions he gathered the entire household on the roof to await this event. He wrote several religious books, including one against swearing. His aversion to swearing was such that he refused to marry his childhood sweetheart when he heard her using bad language. He died a bachelor.

CLERKLAND BRIG & OLD CASTLE. STEWARTON.

Ravenscraig Castle, to the right of centre, has been a ruin for many centuries. Before that it was the residence of the Cunninghames of Corsehill and Auchenharvie. Originally it was the property of Godfrey de Ross, who was granted the land by his overlord Hugh De Morville, the founder of Kilwinning Abbey in 1140.

CORSEHILL BANKS, STEWARTON

B-3239

The Corsehill banks, like those of the Annick, were popular spots for picnics and for children to play. Older residents of Stewarton remember these places as a children's paradise. Well-known bathing haunts of the Corsehill burn were the Auld Dam and the Munt. The Annick had 'Andra Sweelzies' and the Ladies' Dookin' Hole. The Auld Dam and the mill lade on the Corsehill Burn supplied the old Corsehill Mills (corn and wool mills), which were situated at the end of the High Street where it met Dean Street.

The house just seen through the trees, Brookwood, was built at the edge of Gameshill in 1898 for John Sim the butcher. The land behind it, on the left of the picture, was laid out as a golf course in 1912. It was opened on 1 June by Provost Sim, who drove the first ball. The terms for members were, gentlemen 12/6 per annum and 7/6 for ladies. Visitors paid 6*d*. per round of 18 holes, but the course only had nine holes, so they were played twice over. The golf club was plagued with trouble from the beginning over the lease of the ground and on one occasion even had to move the clubhouse at short notice. When another nine holes were laid out on the other side of the Cutstraw Road, members could enjoy an 18-hole course, but this did not last long. In the 1930s the club had only the new nine-hole course, but membership flourished at that time. The war put an end to golf in Stewarton for the duration and afterwards the only land available was at Lochridge where members made do with a very rough course. Even this proved impossible to keep and no golf was played in Stewarton after 1948. Houses were later built on the land at Gameshill. The area of water in the foreground was the dam on the Annick (on the west side of the Holm Street bridge) from which a lade led off water for the Lainshaw Mill.

Mrs Bowie's shop was in Lainshaw Street at the Cross. Her daughter Jenny married David Sim, and after his death ran Sim's bonnet factory at Nether Robertland Mill with her brother Norrie Bowie.

Robert Watt (right), the Stewarton haulage contractor, and employee Mr Thomson, with his steam wagon at Lainshaw gates. The son of a farmer, Watt was more interested in farm machinery than in agriculture itself and went to the Highland Show in Aberdeen to buy his first steam engine in 1916. He started Stewarton's first haulage business, serving the needs of local farmers who did not own their own machinery. He soon added a wagon, followed by tractors and ploughs. He was the first person in the area to own a hammer mill, bought from Toronto at the start of the war, which he used to grind corn into meal as part of the local war effort. He modified the hammer mill to enable it to be transported and from then on took it around the local farms. At one time he used it to grind up broken Penguin biscuits which were then fed to chickens in the form of meal. Robert Watt continued in business until the mid-1960s.

The Stewarton Clothing Work Party at Lainshaw House where they met under the aegis of Mrs Arthur of Lainshaw. In 1915 clothes made by the Stewarton Work Party were sent to the British Red Cross, the Serbian Red Cross, the Antwerp British Hospital Fund, the Navy, prisoners of war in Germany, and various other groups at home and abroad. In April 1915 the Work Party were proud to announce that they had made and despatched 575 pairs of socks, 165 day shirts, 10 night shirts, 16 Navy shirts, 2 pairs of pyjamas, 2 nightrobes, 12 bed jackets, 12 helmets, 4 children's nightgowns, 35 body belts, 35 scarves, 60 pairs of mitts and gloves and 46 sets of vests and pants. In addition many similar articles were donated, along with tobacco, cigarettes, soap, candles, books, bandages and other comforts. The *Kilmarnock Standard* reported that 'it is indeed a remarkable record of industry when one considers that most of the helpers have had a very busy time with Government work'.

The Stewarton Sphagnum Moss Work Party, also photographed at Lainshaw. For the purpose of surgical dressings, Sphagnum moss, gathered from moorland and from countryside abundant in streams, was found to be just as absorbent as conventional materials such as cotton wool which had become scarce and expensive. The workers carefully picked out stalks of grass, sticks and leaves from the moss before wringing out the water. They then spread it out on sheets or nets to dry, and later put it into small muslin bags to make dressings. These were sent to the War Dressing Supply Centre where they were sterilised before being sent to hospitals such as the Scottish Women's Hospital at Rouen.

The Stewarton Bowling Club was founded officially by Robert Mackie in 1861, but bowls are believed to have been played in the town before that. The bowling green, in Dunlop Street, is on a steeply sloping site and was originally on the outskirts of the town. The town, however, has now grown up to meet and surround it. A new clubhouse was built in 1922 and was replaced again in the 1970s, since when it has been extended. The bowler on the far left is John Roberton, and next to him is James Ferguson; on the far right is Robert Mackie, and next to him is (probably) Mr Bowers, one-time janitor of Stewarton Public School.

Members of the Stewarton Bowling Club. From left to right: Mr Bowers (?), unknown, James Ferguson, unknown, Robert Mackie, unknown, Jim Picken (?), and John Roberton (known locally as 'the General').

Stewarton won the Scottish Bowling Association Championship in 1907. The winning team were, from left to right, John Cuthbertson, Alex Dunlop, James Ferguson and John Roberton. The *Kilmarnock Standard* reported: 'A great reception was accorded the conquering heroes at Stewarton. The populace was at the station awaiting their arrival on Saturday evening and along with the crowd was the Burgh Band. When the victorious quartette arrived the band struck up "See the Conquering Heroes Come", and led a procession through the town where enthusiasm was at a great pitch.' After a congratulatory speech and toast at the bowling green by the club's president, Mr J. L. Mackie, 'the proceedings closed upon midnight'.

Robertland House was designed in 1820 by David Hamilton for Alexander Kerr, a Stewarton man and Glasgow tobacco lord. In March 1914, while lying empty and waiting for a buyer, it was set on fire by suffragettes. The Kilmarnock fire brigade was summoned and finding that they could not get sufficient pressure for their hoses from the nearby Annick on much lower ground, they utilised a reservoir situated behind and above the house by cutting through the dam and running the water down an old overflow channel. A newspaper report told how 'with a double length of hose many thousand gallons of water were thrown on the blazing building' and the firemen managed to contain and then extinguish the flames. They prevented the fire from spreading to the large rear wing of the house and the outbuildings, but the whole of the front of the building had been gutted. Evidence of the identity of the perpetrators was found in the driveway in the form of two postcards, bearing the messages: 'Release Mrs Pankhurst' and 'This has been done owing to the dastardly outrage on Mrs Pankhurst on Monday. Now is the time for the Church to show its independence of the State. R.I.P.' The damage was restored soon after the fire.

It was through a window in the conservatory at Robertland House that the two suffragettes gained access to the house to set fire to it. According to the newspaper report, 'the glass was carefully removed and the pieces laid on the ground close by . . . and once inside the conservatory they easily forced the door leading to the house'. Two sets of footprints were later traced through some fields to the Glasgow road.

Dunlop Road Lugton

Looking towards Lugton from the Dunlop road, this view is from the first of Lugton's two railway bridges (now partly demolished), near the old 'High' or 'Cally' Station from which passengers could travel to Neilston and beyond in one direction and to Ardrossan in the other. The line was opened in 1888 and the line to Irvine and Ardrossan was closed in 1964. The cottages on the left were occupied by railway workers and still stand but have been greatly altered. Just past them the white cottage is the old toll house. Across the road is the former stationmaster's house. Beyond it can be seen buildings of the station. Also in this area was the jam factory, known locally as the Lugton Jeely Works, which were next to Craigholm House and owned by John Muir and family. Muir's made jam in Lugton from 1912 until 1928. Their speciality was rhubarb jam and other fruits were brought by train; some people said that the jam got its distinctive flavour from the addition of turnips.

Lugton's other station, on the Glasgow and Kilmarnock Joint Railway's line, was entered by the road through the white gates. The line was opened in 1873 and brought expansion and prosperity to Lugton. It came from Glasgow via Nitshill, Barrhead and Caldwell and went on to Dunlop, Stewarton, Kilmaurs and Kilmarnock. There was a branch line to Beith. The stationmaster's house is on the left, facing the main road, and railway worker's cottages are in a row behind it.

The Lugton Inn is recorded in the *New Statistical Account* of 1845: 'A very respectable inn has been built at Lugton bridge, on the road from Irvine to Glasgow. Besides this there are six houses in which spiritous liquors are sold. One-half of them might, with benefit to the public, be suppressed.'

The row of cottages facing the Glasgow road was built to accommodate around 200 workers at the iron ore mines of Merry and Cunninghame. When the iron ore was worked out, brickworks were established in the late 1890s to make use of the blaes bings, by-products of the iron works. Lugton bricks were used for most of the local buildings built between 1890 and 1921. The cottages in the photograph still stand, although some of them have been altered. The row originally extended further to the north (left of picture). After the brickworks were closed in 1921 they were occupied by local people and one of the cottages (in the second block from the left) was a post office. The cottage at the end of the row before the detached one was a garage which flourished under the ownership of the Robertson family for many years.

The Lugton Water flows under the bridge between the Lugton Inn and the old smithy. The building on the right was a barn belonging to the Inn which was burned down. The cottage on the left still stands and behind it can be seen the old smithy.

There has been a church in Dunlop since the twelfth century. The present church was built in 1835 and incorporates part of two previous churches, one – the north aisle, visible here – dating to 1641 and holding the burial vault of the Dunlops; it was rebuilt in 1766, but by the 1830s was no longer big enough to accommodate the increased population. The new church was described in 1845 as 'a handsome and commodious edifice, capable of accommodating about 750 persons', and at that time it was still the only place of worship in the village. The first Protestant minister at Dunlop was Hans Hamilton who was created Viscount Clandeboye by James VI. He and his wife are buried in a vault behind Clandeboyes Hall, situated beside the church to the south.

DUNLOP, PARISH CHURCH & ST.

The village of Dunlop in the late eighteenth century consisted chiefly of these cottages built here between the church and the manse, in the area known as the Kirktoun, between 1751 and 1782. The bottom of the hill is known as the Townfoot. At the reunion of the churches in 1929 it was decided that the Parish Church would be known as the Laigh Church, to distinguish it from the former United Free Church higher up the village.

Allan Gilmour's stores originally occupied both halves of this building, as shown here. Later the right hand part became a hosiery shop and Gilmour's was confined to the other half. The post office, first opened in Dunlop in 1852, was housed in the late nineteenth century in part of the house next to Gilmour's. Next to it and set back a little is the school (hardly visible in this photograph) with the schoolmaster's house next to it. The cottage next to the schoolhouse once housed Mrs Peacock's haberdashery.

School and School House, Dunlop

The school was built in 1876 in response to the Education Act of 1872, replacing the school on the opposite side of the street which had served the parish from 1837. It was altered and extended in 1931. Dunlop had had one since 1641, when James, Viscount Clandeboye, opened a school in Clandeboyes Hall.

The High Church was built in 1845 as a Free Church and later became the United Free. It became known as the High Church when it entered the Union with the Church of Scotland. The congregations of Dunlop's two churches were joined in the early 1960s and this building became the church hall. On the far left of the photograph Mrs Bull's sweet shop can be seen.

Dunlop Public Hall was built in 1891 after the sum of £762. 1s. 6d. was raised by a grand bazaar at Dunlop House in the summer of 1890. It had a main hall and a reading or billiards room which could be opened up to extend the main hall and offer accommodation for 400. The hall was opened on 8 December 1891, with a 'grand concert', presided over by Major Dalrymple of Dunlop House. Various speakers recounted the stages by which the hall had come into being, everyone was thanked and several performers gave musical renditions from the platform. The *Kilmarnock Standard* was able to report that 'the proceedings altogether passed off with great *éclat*'. In the 1920s a large extension was built in brick. The driveway beside it was later opened up as a public roadway and is now Kirkland Road. A village war memorial was erected in front of the hall, but was moved to the churchyard in the 1960s.

This view of Hapland House (on the left) is from the Stewarton Road near the railway bridge. William Sommerville established Hapland Mill, a blanket mill, on the Glazert where a mill lade and dam supplied the power. In 1896 Thomas Mackie, of the dyeing and spinning business, moved here from Stewarton, took over the mill and continued the blanket weaving business on his own account. In 1919 Hapland Mill was amalgamated with the family business of Thomas Mackie and Sons and continued to spin wool and weave blankets until 1940, when under war zoning regulations blanket production moved elsewhere. It continued as a spinning mill, but was burned down in the early 1980s. The house still stands but the view of it from here is now partially obscured by trees.

OLD MILL WHEEL DUNLOP

There were five corn mills in Dunlop parish in 1840. The Old Mill was owned by James Anderson and was destroyed by fire in 1862. Some traces of the masonry still remain, near where the Commoncraig path crosses the Glazert.

Bridgend, Dunlop 322/6

The old bridge over the Black Burn at Bridgend still exists, but the road (on the right from Townfoot towards Beith) now crosses a new bridge to the left of this one. The cottage no longer stands and poultry houses now occupy the site. The trees can be recognised today. This photograph, dating from around 1926, is taken near the entrance to an old whinstone quarry. The Dunlop area is rich in blue whinstone which was transported to Glasgow by rail from 1873 onwards for the growing city's paving needs.

WEST LODGE, DUNLOP HOUSE, DUNLOP.

Dunlop House was designed in 1831–34 by David Hamilton for Sir James Dunlop of Dunlop, whose family had held the estate and castle for many centuries. The house is built in an unusual Scottish-Jacobean style, but the gate lodge is in a style more typical of Hamilton, with classical and manorial features, and more of the strap work decoration that adorns the house.

VIEW IN DUNLOP HO...

The grounds of Dunlop House were *en fête* on Friday 18 and Saturday 19 July 1890. According to the *Kilmarnock Standard* 'never was there a more enjoyable or successful undertaking' than the Grand Fancy Fair and Bazaar held to raise money to build a public hall for Dunlop, under the patronage of Major and Mrs Dalrymple. The Stewarton Instrumental Band was in attendance, and 'theatrical and ventriloquial entertainments and concerts of vocal music' were performed in a large marquee, and 'a varied and excellent bill of fare was furnished in another marquee'. The bazaar was held in the house itself and there was rifle shooting and an 'Aunt Sally' in the grounds. Towards evening the unused eatables from the refreshment tent were auctioned, the various lots 'reaching almost bazaar prices'. Mr Cochrane of the Railway Hotel, Stewarton, ran brakes every hour from Stewarton, and from every train arriving at Dunlop Station, during the two days.

32218 Dunlop Bowling Green

Dunlop Bowling Club was opened on 11 June 1927, the ceremony performed by Mrs T. Watson of Dunlop House. Over 100 members subscribed, including 25 ladies. Annual subscriptions were 21 shillings for gentlemen, and half of that for ladies. The green, near the railway station, was made largely by the voluntary efforts of local people, and the local farmers transported around 1,000 tons of stones, ashes and sand free of charge for its foundations and bottoming. The clubhouse was built by Messrs Robert Howie and Sons.